ISBN 0-7683-2027-5

Elvis and Elvis Presley are Registered Trademarks of
Elvis Presley Enterprises, Inc.
© 1997 Elvis Presley Enterprises, Inc.

Published in 1998 by Cedco Publishing Company,
100 Pelican Way, San Rafael, CA 94901.

Printed in Hong Kong

All rights reserved. No part of this publication may be
reproduced, stored in a retrieval system or transmitted in any
form or by any means, electronic, mechanical, photocopying,
recording or otherwise, without the prior written
permission of the publisher.

For a free full-color catalog,
please write us at the address above
or visit our website: www.cedco.com

1 3 5 7 9 10 8 6 4 2

Elvis and his Parents

This early Presley family portrait (1938) shows three-year old Elvis with his parents Gladys Love Smith Presley and Vernon Elvis Presley. Elvis was born January 8, 1935 in Tupelo, Mississippi, in the midst of the Great Depression, to poverty-stricken parents. Nobody could have anticipated that the greatest recording artist in history would have come from such inauspicious beginnings.

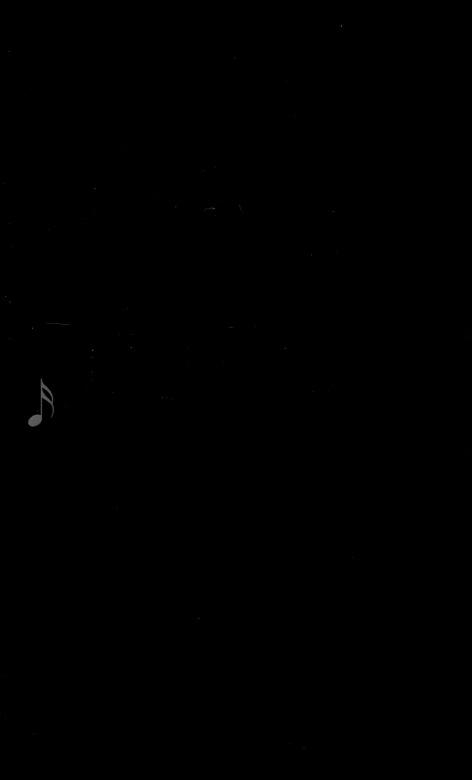

Where it All Began

The birthplace of Elvis, a two-room clapboard house in Tupelo, Mississippi, was commemorated by a fan in this painting. Vernon and Gladys Presley had been living with Vernon's parents in Tupelo, when they discovered Gladys was expecting. Vernon and his brother Vester built the 15-by-30 foot house at 306 Old Saltillo Road so the family could have their own home. They lived there for several years. The site is now a museum.

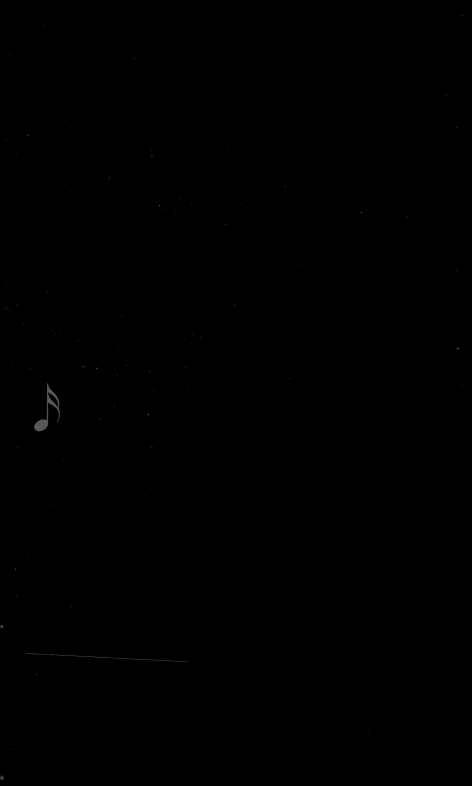

The Hillbilly Cat

This photo shows a 1955 concert appearance. Elvis' career had ignited in late 1954 with regular appearances on *Louisiana Hayride* and gigs at nightclubs, roadhouses, auditoriums, and fairgrounds throughout the South. On May 13, 1955, at a concert in Jacksonville Florida, a riot ensued as Elvis ended his performance with the playful quip, "I'll see you all backstage, girls." Teenage girls tore most of his clothes off that night as they rushed the dressing room. It was the first but not the last of such incidents.

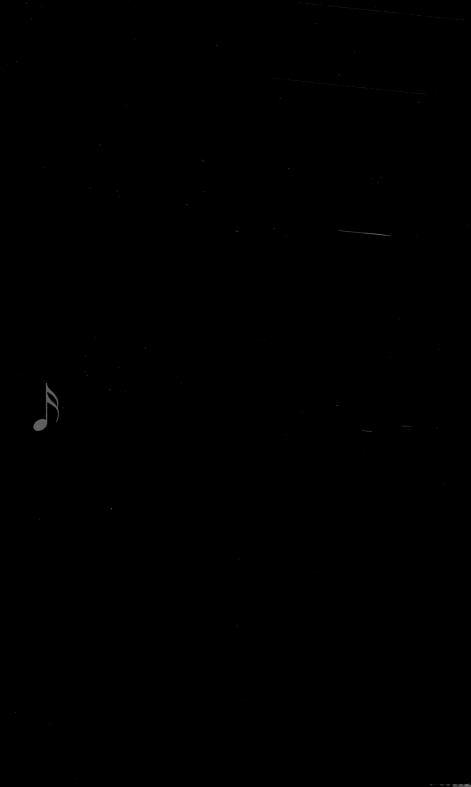

Hound Dog

Elvis with two bloodhounds in a publicity shot. When Elvis first performed the song on TV on the *Milton Berle Show*, June 5, 1956 there was public outcry over the implicit sexuality in his delivery. When Elvis appeared on the *Steve Allen Show* less than a month later, he was presented in a tuxedo singing the hit to a basset hound.

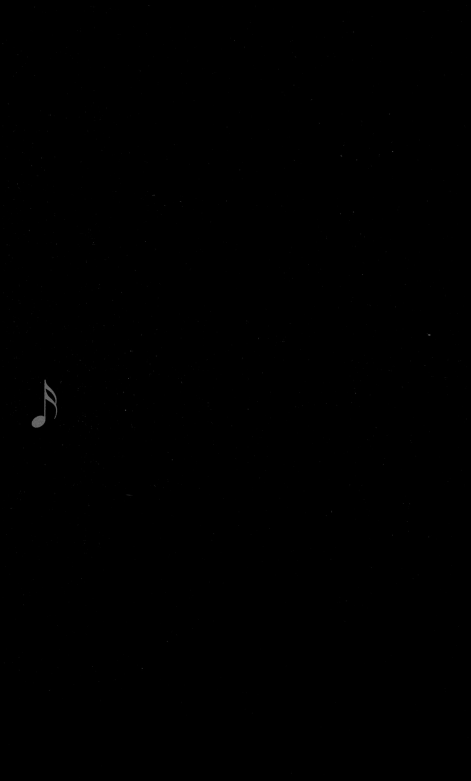

The First Gold Record

"Heartbreak Hotel," released January 27, 1956 with "I Was the One" on the B-side, became the first Elvis single to sell more than one million copies. This gold record, the first of many, is displayed in the trophy room at Graceland.

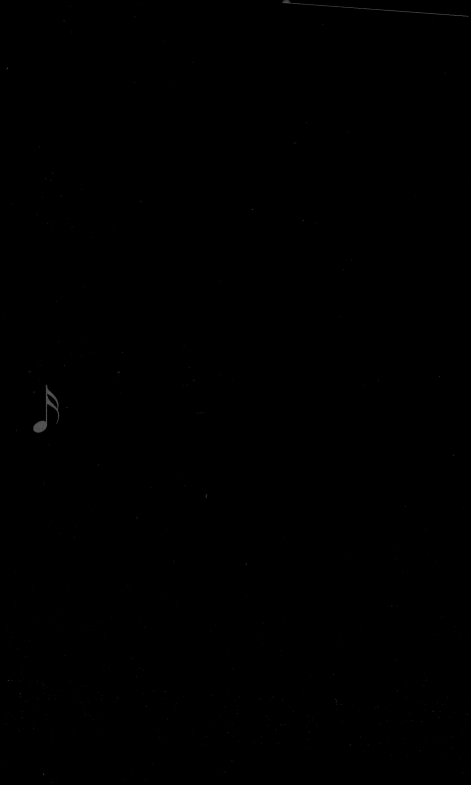

Elvis in Vegas for the First Time

Elvis poses for a publicity shot in front of the New Frontier Hotel in Las Vegas in this photo. His engagement, which began April 23, 1956 was supposed to have lasted four weeks, but the older audiences didn't identify with the sensational young singer and the booking was canceled after two weeks. When Elvis returns to Vegas thirteen years later, his shows break house records.

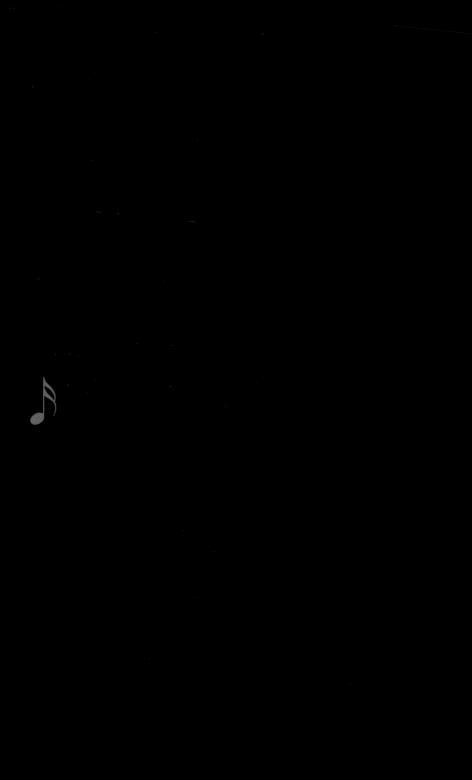

Elvis On Top

This 1956 publicity photo, portrays the sexy, sultry, quintessential Elvis. 1956 was a landmark year in his career, with his first gold record single, his first gold record album, his first national TV appearance (on *Stage Show*), his record-breaking performance on *Ed Sullivan*—seen by 53 million viewers, and his first movie role in *Love Me Tender*.

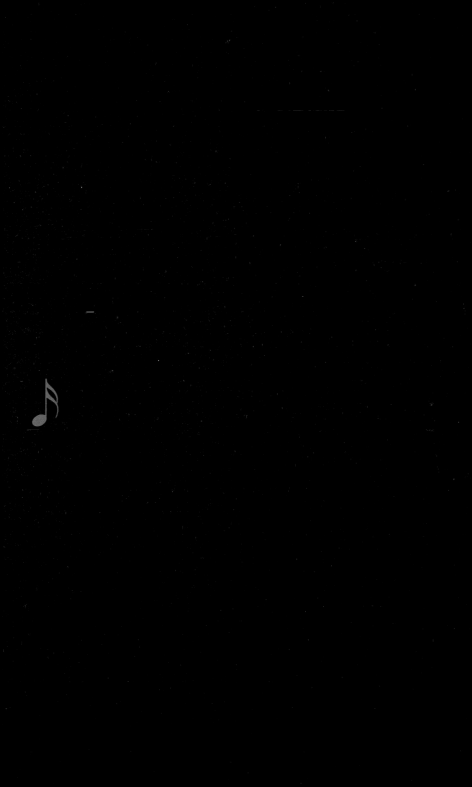

Elvis Embarks on His Movie Career

Elvis on the set of *Love Me Tender*. This 1956 Twentieth Century Fox film launched Elvis' movie career, which spanned 16 years and produced 33 films. Among the more memorable are *Jailhouse Rock*, *Loving You*, *King Creole*, *Blue Hawaii*, and *Viva Las Vegas*. Elvis was one of the highest-paid and most bankable stars in Hollywood for a number of years.

Elvis Giving Back

Elvis wears the jacket from his famous gold lamé suit designed by Nudie's of Hollywood during a benefit performance for a Tupelo youth center. Elvis generously devoted time, energy, and money to numerous charities in Tupelo, Memphis and elsewhere. In 1970, Elvis was named One of the Ten Outstanding Young Men of the Nation by the U.S. Jaycees—one of the criteria being service to humanity. The award was an honor Elvis was deeply proud of.

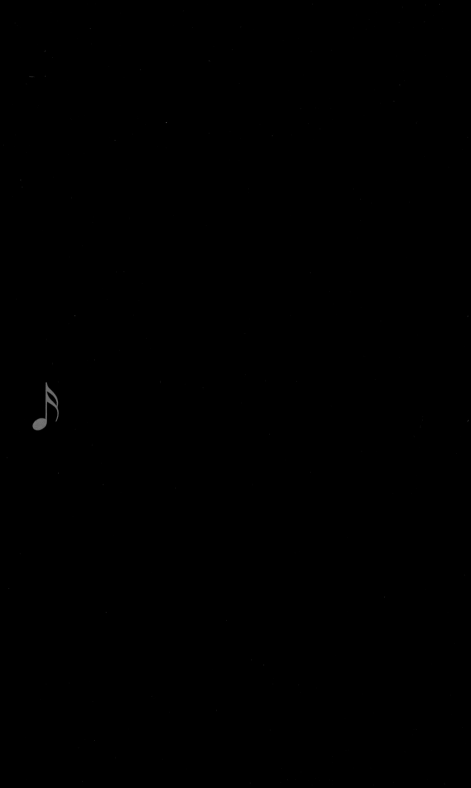

Love, Elvis

Always happy to accommodate his fans, Elvis signs autographs during a break in the filming of *Loving You*. This 1957 Paramount picture was the star's second film and included the hits "Teddy Bear" and "Loving You." The soundtrack album went gold.

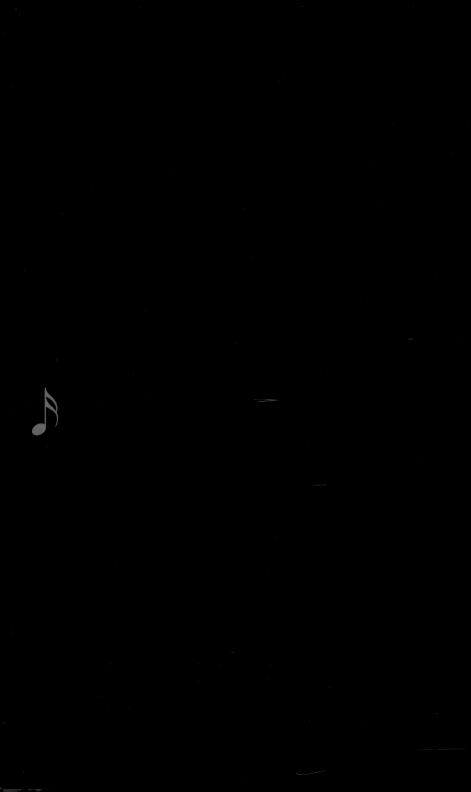

Memorabilia of the King of Rock and Roll

A showcase in the trophy room at Graceland featuring early Elvis memorabilia, such as his gold lamé suit—arguably the most famous performance costume in entertainment history—and a favorite Gibson J-200 guitar.

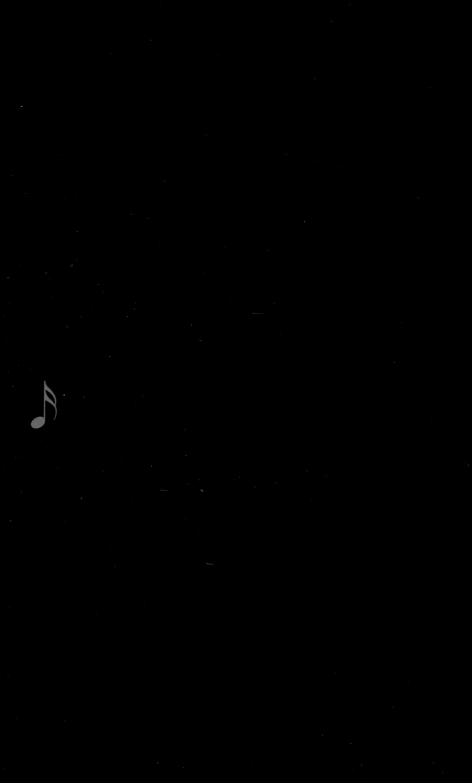

Souvenir Candid

Making the most of their photo opportunity, these two fans capture Elvis in his 1956 purple Cadillac outside the Graceland gates, in 1957. Elvis gave a lot to his fans and in turn, Elvis' fans were, and are, the most devoted of all.

Soldier Elvis

Even as Elvis served his country in the Army, music was still integral to his life. This photo shows him at his home off-base in Germany in 1959, toward the end of his military career. Elvis, however, declined to enter the Special Services branch of the Army, wherein his duties would be entertaining the troops; instead he served as a regular G.I. By the time his service ended, he had earned the rank of sergeant.

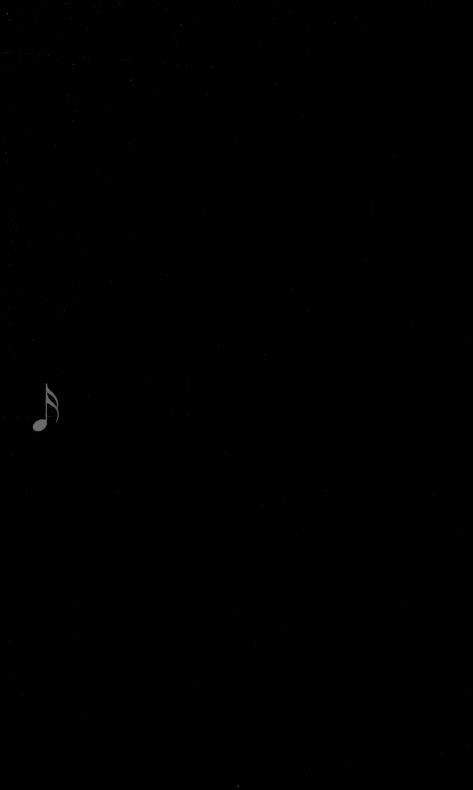

Elvis performing during Frank Sinatra's "Welcome Home, Elvis" television special in 1960. One of the show's highlights was Elvis and Old Blue Eyes singing a duet of "Love Me Tender." During the time Elvis was serving in Germany, Colonel Parker had confirmed his masterful promotions and RCA had been releasing songs Elvis had recorded before he left. When Elvis returned, his career was intact and he had more fans than ever.

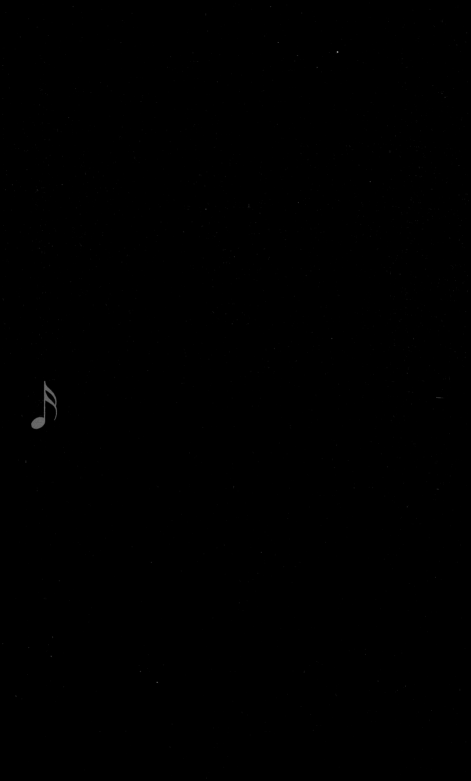

Elvis in Hawaii for a Benefit

1961-a contemplative Elvis looks out from the hotel balcony, shortly after arriving in Hawaii to perform a benefit to raise funds for the building of the U.S.S. Arizona Memorial, a WW II monument. A year later, the Memorial was completed. Elvis was notably generous in his contributions to charity and worthy causes.

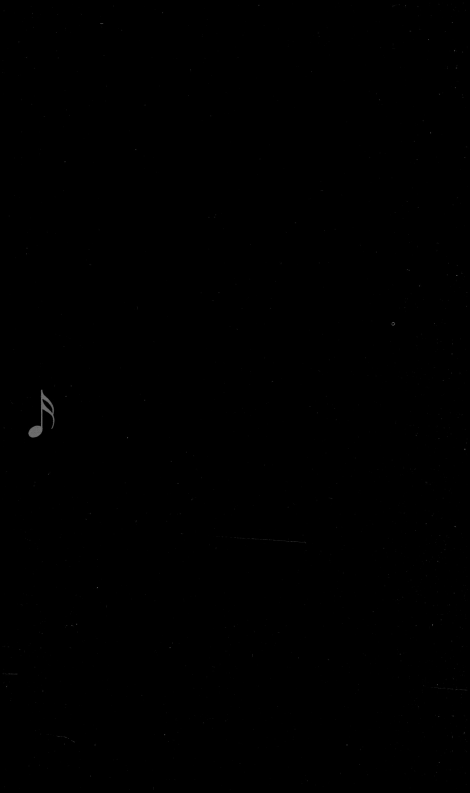

Graceland, Home of the King of Rock and Roll

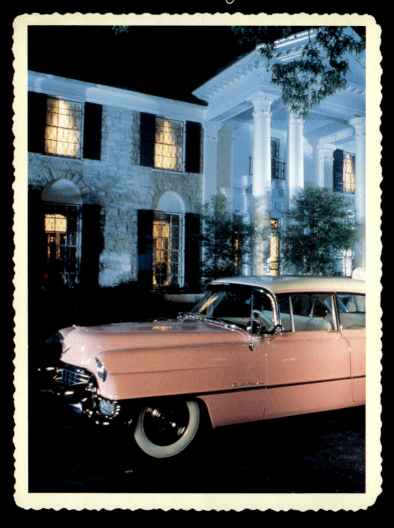

Elvis' famous 1955 pink Cadillac Fleetwood sedan parked in front of Graceland, the mansion he bought for $100,000 in March 1957. Purchasing Graceland fulfilled Elvis' lifelong dream of providing his parents a fine home. It also served as his personal refuge from the pressures of fame. Today, over 700,000 people tour Graceland each year.

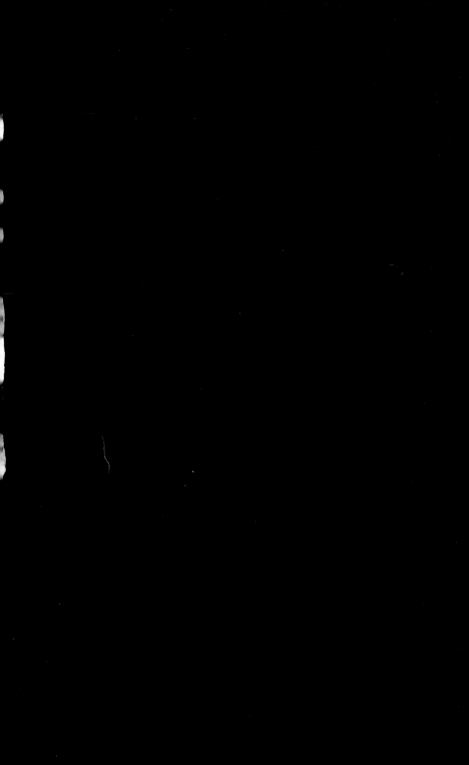